DISCOVER THE KIND OF LOVE
YOUR SOUL CAME TO REMEMBER

TWIN FLAME

SOULMATE

OR

MONAD

A REFLECTIVE GUIDE TO RECOGNIZE YOUR SOUL CONNECTION

GRACE BREWSTER

Copyright © 2025 Grace Brewster

All rights reserved. No part of this book may be reproduced, distributed, or transmitted in any form or by any means, including photocopying, recording, or other electronic or mechanical methods, without the prior written permission of the publisher, except in the case of brief quotations embodied in critical reviews and certain other noncommercial uses permitted by copyright law.

First Edition: 2025
ISBN: 978-1-0698207-9-2
Self Published

Facebook: Grace Brewster Author
Instagram: @cosmiclovethebook

This book is a work of reflection. It is intended for personal insight and inspiration. The author is not providing medical, psychological, or legal advice, and readers should seek professional guidance where appropriate.

DEDICATION

For every soul
who has ever searched for love
and discovered it was never lost.

For the ones who loved bravely,
let go gracefully,
and remembered quietly.

And for those still walking home,
may these pages be a light
on the path you already know.

Acknowledgments

With gratitude to the quiet forces that guide every word, to the unseen teachers, both in spirit and in human form, who remind us that love continues to evolve through us all.

To the readers walking this path of remembrance, thank you for allowing these reflections to be part of your own unfolding.

And to everyone who holds light in their own way through kindness, truth, and presence, this book is for you.

Table of Contents

CHAPTER

FROM THE AUTHOR'S HEART
AUTHOR'S NOTE
1. Love in Many Forms
2. Soulmates, Twin Flames, and the Monad
3. When the Connection Feels Effortless
4. Shared Lessons, Past Lives, and Healing Contracts
5. When It's Time to Let Go
6. The Magnetic Pull You Can't Explain
7. The Mirror Effect: Why It Hurts
8. Separation, Silence, And Surrender
9. Activation and Awakening
10. Mission Energy: When Love Becomes Purpose
11. Soulmates: Harmony and Healing
12. Kindred Spirits
13. Family as Soul Agreements
14. Animals and Earth Allies
15. When Soulmates Depart
16. Beyond The Mirror
17. Integration of Love
18. The Silence of Union
19. Embodying the Monad
20. Wholeness

CHAPTER

21. Balancing Polarity
22. Healing Attachment
23. The Path of Surrender
24. Reunion Through Self-Love
25. Beyond Reunion: Living the Mission

FINAL REFLECTION
AFTERWORD REFLECTION
EPILOGUE

From the Author's Heart

Every book I've written began as a conversation with love.
Sometimes love spoke through joy.
Sometimes through silence.
Sometimes through loss so deep
it felt like the universe was erasing me
only to draw me again in light.

This book is not about me,
it's about us.
Every soul who has ever searched, surrendered, healed, and remembered.
Every reader who has looked for meaning in connection,
and discovered that love was never leaving,
only evolving.

We are all students and teachers of the same truth:
that love is not a destination,
but a frequency that lives within.

If these pages reached you,
it's because your own heart was ready to remember.
And if you take anything from this journey,
let it be this:

You are not here to be perfect.
You are here to be present.
To love with awareness.
To live with intention.
To walk as a soul who remembers.

May this book remind you
that you never lost the light,
you only forgot where you placed it.

Keep choosing love.
Not because it's easy,
but because it's who you are.

With all my heart,
 Grace Brewster

Author's Note

How to travel through this book

This book is written as a journey, not just to read, but to experience.
Each part represents a stage of remembrance, from the human heart to the soul's awakening and finally to the living embodiment of love itself.

Part I. The Many Faces of Connection
Explores love in its most personal form; the joys, fears, and attachments that shape our earliest understanding of connection.

Part II. The Twin Flame
Dives into the sacred fire of awakening; the mirror that challenges, expands, and ultimately transforms the self.

Part III. Soulmates & Sacred Companions
Softens the journey, showing love as peace, friendship, and resonance through many forms of connection.

Part IV. The Monad: The One Soul
Is the remembering where separation dissolves, and we recognize that all love leads back to the same source.

Part V. Living the Lesson
Is the embodiment, the practice of carrying that wholeness into everyday life.
It's where love becomes how we walk, not just what we seek.

You can read the book straight through or intuitively open to the section that calls to you most.
Each chapter is complete on its own, yet all are threads of one tapestry, the soul's return to unity.

Take these words as invitations, not instructions.
Your path may look different, but the destination is the same, the quiet knowing that you have always been love itself.

INTRODUCTION

The journey back to the one

Every love story is a mirror.
Some reflect our wounds,
some our strength,
and a few, the rare ones, reflect our soul.

We meet people who awaken us,
others who comfort us,
and some who break us open so completely
that light rushes through the cracks.
Each encounter is a teacher.
Each chapter of love is a classroom of remembrance.

This book was born from that remembering,
the understanding that love is not a search outside of us,
but a sacred unfolding within.

The twin flame taught us about awakening,
the soulmate taught us about harmony,
and the Monad teaches us about wholeness,
the return to the single consciousness
that has always been breathing us.

You don't have to know every metaphysical term or believe in destiny to read these pages.
You only have to have loved deeply enough to wonder why, bravely enough to learn, and softly enough to listen.

The chapters ahead are not rules; they're reflections.
Each one is an open doorway into a different facet of love's evolution
from human attachment to divine embodiment.

Take your time with them.
Let them breathe between your days.
Pause when a line stirs something familiar.
That stirring is your soul remembering itself.

You are not here to chase union.
You are here to become it.
To live love not as a longing,
but as a state of being —
grounded, gentle, awake.

May these words meet you where you are
and guide you home to where you've always been.

Part I

The Many Faces of Connection

CHAPTER 1

Love in Many Forms

Love does not arrive in only one costume.

It can enter your life as a partner, a friend, a stranger on a plane, or a sudden memory that moves you to tears.

Each form is an echo of the same Source trying to meet itself through you.

We were taught that love should look a certain way: mutual, lasting, and safe.

But the soul plays by different rules. It seeks experience, expansion, remembrance.

Sometimes love comes to teach you courage.
Sometimes it comes to help you release control.

And sometimes it simply passes through to remind you that your heart can still feel.

Not all loves are meant to stay. Some are doorways.

They open you to a new frequency, then quietly close when their lesson is complete.

The human self calls this loss.
The soul calls it movement.

Each connection is sacred because it awakens a part of you that was asleep.

Whether it lasts a lifetime or a single season, its purpose is the same: to guide you closer to yourself.

When you begin to see love this way, not as possession but as reflection, you stop measuring it by time or outcome.

You begin to recognize that every love, in every form, has already served you perfectly.

Reflection:

Love wears many faces.
Sometimes it arrives as friendship,
sometimes as passion,
and sometimes as a lesson wrapped in loss.

It is never limited to romance;
it is the pulse that connects all things.

Take a moment to look back on the forms love has taken in your life:
a kind word, a quiet moment, a presence that held space for you.
Each expression was love,
shaped differently,
but born of the same light.

Ask yourself:
How have I defined love,
and how might life be gentler
if I allowed it to appear in every form?

When you see love everywhere,
You stop searching for it,
you begin to live it.

Chapter 2

Soulmates, Twin Flames, and the Monad

We are souls within souls, threads of the same vast tapestry.

Each of us belongs to a greater soul family, and within that family are distinct patterns of connection.

Some appear as gentle companions who walk beside us for comfort.
Others ignite us so completely that our entire inner world shifts in their presence.

A soulmate is the familiar echo of someone whose energy feels like home.
They arrive to share, to heal, and to remind you that you are never truly alone in this world.

Soulmates may be friends, partners, or even brief acquaintances who touch your heart and vanish like a breeze.

They offer peace and support not to complete you, but to mirror the harmony you've begun to anchor within yourself.

A twin flame, however, is different.

It is the magnetic pull of the same soul, divided into two bodies, two lives, two timelines.

When you meet them, something ancient stirs.

It is not about romance, though it can appear that way.

It is about remembrance, a contract to awaken one another through love, pain, and surrender.

You are each other's catalyst, mirror, and fire.

Where a soulmate soothes, a twin flame shatters, so that only truth remains.

And beyond both, there is the Monad, the greater Self from which all these soul sparks originate.

Think of it as the sun and each of us as its rays.

Within the Monad, there are countless aspects of your own consciousness exploring different paths, bodies, and lessons.

You, your twin, your soulmates, all of you are expressions of that same Oversoul seeking to know itself through infinite experience.

When you remember this, the labels begin to soften.

It matters less who they are to you and more what they awaken within you.*

Because in truth, every connection is the Monad meeting itself, love encountering love through the illusion of separation.

Realization Space

- Which connections in my life feel like peace, and which feel like fire?
- Can I honor both as sacred expressions of the same love?

REFLECTION

Love takes many forms,
but all are threads of one tapestry.

Some souls come to walk beside you in harmony.
Some arrive to mirror your growth.
And beyond them all exists the Monad,
the source where every soul returns to oneness.

Each connection leads you closer to remembrance:
that love was never between two;
 it was always within the One.

Close your eyes and reflect:
Which connections in your life have opened your heart the most?
Which have challenged you to expand beyond your limits?

Every encounter, joyful or painful,
has been guiding you toward the same realization —

that you were never separate to begin with.

Chapter 3

When the Connection Feels Effortless

Some connections unfold like breathing.

You don't have to chase, convince, or perform. There's an ease that feels like home, not because it's dramatic or intense, but because your soul recognizes safety.

Soul mates often feel this way. The bond carries familiarity and comfort because you've shared lifetimes of harmony or healing. The energy flows smoothly, lessons are learned gently, not through fire.

If you're constantly at peace rather than in crisis, you may be with a soul mate. These relationships remind you what love feels like when it's balanced, not perfect, but peaceful.

REFLECTION

Some connections feel like breathing —
natural, easy, familiar.
There's no need to explain, prove, or perform.
You simply recognize each other,
and peace follows.

Effortless connections remind you
that love doesn't always arrive through struggle.
Sometimes it comes as rest,
a remembering of what was always whole.

Take a quiet moment to feel into those bonds in your life.
Who brings you calm just by existing?
Who reminds you that love can be gentle?

Effortless love teaches balance.
It whispers, "You don't have to earn what already belongs to you."

Chapter 4

Shared Lessons, Past Lives, and Healing Contracts

Every connection holds purpose, but soul mates often come to fulfill agreements made long before you met.

Perhaps one of you once abandoned the other, and now you return to learn forgiveness.

Once you silence your truth, you come together to find your voice.

These are not punishments. They are sacred exchanges, where souls help each other grow through grace instead of chaos.

When the lesson completes, the energy softens. Sometimes you stay together, sometimes you lovingly part.

REFLECTION

Every soul you meet has walked with you before —
in another time, another form, another story.
Together you return, again and again,
to finish what was left incomplete,
to heal what once divided you,
to remember love in deeper ways.

Not all meetings are meant to last,
but all are meant to teach.

Close your eyes and think of someone
whose presence has challenged or changed you.
What lesson might your souls have chosen to explore this time?
What healing could be waiting beneath the surface?

When you view your connections through the eyes of eternity,
judgment softens into gratitude.
You realize: no meeting was random,
only beautifully timed.

Chapter 5

When It's Time to Let Go

Not every connection is meant to last forever, but every connection is meant to awaken something in you.

When the energy starts to feel heavy, when growth turns into resistance, the soul may be signaling completion.

Letting go doesn't mean the love was false. It means the lesson is integrated.

The relationship fulfilled its contract, and the next part of your path requires space.

Grieve what was, bless what it gave, and release what no longer flows.

REFLECTION

Letting go isn't the end of love,
it's the release of attachment,
the trust that what's meant to return will find its way.

Some souls walk with you for a lifetime,
others only long enough to open a door inside you.
When the moment comes to part,
it isn't failure — it's completion.

Take a deep breath.
Think of someone you've had to release with love.
What gifts did they leave behind?
What parts of you did their presence awaken?

Letting go means keeping the lesson
and freeing the form.
It's how the soul makes space
for new light to enter.

Part II

The Twin Flame Path

Chapter 6

The Magnetic Pull You Can't Explain

When you meet your twin flame, something inside you remembers long before the mind understands.

It isn't an attraction in the ordinary sense. It's recognition.
The eyes meet, and lifetimes collapse.

Your whole body hums with an ancient code that says, Here you are.

You try to reason with it, compare it to chemistry, destiny, timing, but none of those words fit.

This kind of pull doesn't ask for permission.
It rearranges the air around you.

At first, it feels like love amplified: familiar, electric, terrifying.
But what's really happening is energy finding itself.

Two aspects of one soul, drawn back into alignment, igniting the memory of what wholeness feels like.

You can't escape the magnet.
You can only learn to hold the current.

Because the purpose of the pull isn't possession—it's awakening.

It draws you not just to the other person, but to the parts of yourself that had been asleep.

REFLECTION

Some connections defy logic.
You meet their eyes,
and the universe rearranges itself.

It isn't attraction in the usual sense,
it's remembrance.
Two frequencies recognizing their shared origin.

That pull isn't meant to trap you;
it's meant to awaken you.
It shows you what's dormant within,
the parts of you that are ready to feel, to remember, to evolve.

Think of the one who pulled your soul wide open.
What did that connection reveal about you?
What did it teach you about the intensity of love and the courage it takes to stay open?

The magnetic pull isn't the destination.
It's the spark that begins your return to yourself.

Chapter 7

The Mirror Effect: Why It Hurts

The twin flame isn't here to complete you.
They're here to reflect you.

Every wound you've buried, every fear you've hidden, every fragment you've disowned;
They'll mirror it back with exquisite precision.
Not to punish, but to purify.
Because love that deep can only survive in truth.

At first, it feels like chaos.
One moment, you're in divine union.
The next, you're triggered, defensive, raw.
You wonder how someone who feels like home could also feel like fire.
But that's the alchemy of the mirror,
it burns away illusion until only the real remains.

The closer you get, the more transparent you become.
Their silence cuts through your expectations.
Their presence awakens your longing.
Their retreat exposes your need for control.

The pain isn't a sign of failure; it's the soul's surgery.
Each confrontation is a chance to meet yourself again,
to say, I see me, even here.

Because when you can love yourself in the reflection that hurts the most,
you begin to master the flame.

And that's when the mirror becomes light.

REFLECTION

The one who mirrors you
isn't here to wound you,
they're here to show you where love still hides.

Pain arises when your reflection reveals
what you've avoided seeing.
But that reflection is the doorway,
not the punishment.

Look gently at what their presence stirs in you.
Is it insecurity? longing? unhealed grief?
Each feeling points to a part of you
asking to be embraced, not erased.

When you can look into the mirror
without flinching or defending,
the lesson transforms into freedom.

Healing begins
when you realize the mirror was never against you,
it was always for you.

Chapter 8

Separation, Silence, and Surrender

Every twin flame journey passes through silence.
It's the space where love is tested and purified.
One soul retreats, the other reaches out, and both ache in the distance they've created.
But silence is not absence.
It's initiation.

The runner isn't running from you.
They're running from the reflection of themselves that your love exposed.
And the chaser isn't chasing them.
They're chasing the feeling of connection that once silenced their own fear.

Eventually, both must stop moving.
Because the only way to end the cycle is to surrender.

Surrender doesn't mean giving up; it means giving in to what's real.
It means trusting the bond even when you can't feel it.
It means releasing control, so love can breathe without conditions.

In the quiet, something softens.
You begin to hear the whispers beneath the pain —
guidance, remembrance, truth.
The energy that once surged toward the other turns inward,
illuminating the places that still need your care.

Separation is where union begins.
Because when you can hold love without needing it to respond,

You rise into the frequency where reunion can find you again.

REFLECTION

Silence can feel like absence,
but sometimes it's the space love needs to breathe.

When the connection grows quiet,
your soul is not being abandoned,
it's being invited inward.

In separation, you learn to listen to your own frequency again.
To find peace without their presence,
to remember who you are beyond the mirror.

Take a moment and breathe into the stillness.
What is this silence teaching you?
What strength is being built in the waiting?

Surrender doesn't mean you've given up.
It means you've stopped resisting what is.
It's how the heart learns to trust the unseen.

Chapter 9

Activation and Awakening

Something shifts after the silence.
You start feeling energy move through you, sometimes like lightning, sometimes like grace.
Your heart expands beyond logic.
You sense their presence in dreams, in songs, in the wind.
It's as if love has rewired your entire being.

This is activation.
The twin flame connection isn't meant to stay only in the human story;
it's meant to awaken the divine memory within both souls.
Your DNA stirs.
Your intuition heightens.
Synchronicities multiply.
It's not an obsession, it's communication on a higher plane.

You begin to understand that what you feel for them is actually your soul awakening to itself.
The love that once seemed between you now flows through YOU.
You realize that separation never truly existed; it was an illusion designed to awaken remembrance.

The more you embody that frequency of unconditional love,
the more your outer reality starts to transform.
You see purpose behind the pain,
and light inside every shadow.

The activation is not something your twin gives you.
They ignite it, but you sustain it.
The flame they lit in you becomes your own torch.
And with it, you begin to walk as consciousness in motion —
awake, aware, and guided by love itself.

REFLECTION

Awakening often begins as disruption,
the moment life stops fitting
into its old shapes.

An activation isn't something you seek;
it finds you.
It's the instant your soul recognizes truth
and refuses to fall asleep again.

Through the one who awakened you,
you met your own light.
Their presence flipped a hidden switch inside you,
and suddenly, everything felt alive.

Take a moment to reflect:
What part of you woke up when they entered your life?
What truths can you no longer ignore?

Awakening isn't the end of dreaming,
it's the moment you realize
you were the dreamer all along.

Chapter 10

Mission Energy: When Love Becomes Purpose

Once the flame is steady inside you, it begins to move outward.
The connection that once consumed you now fuels your service.
You no longer ask, "When will they come back?"
You ask, "What am I here to create?"

This is mission energy,
when love matures from longing into embodiment.
Your heart becomes a transmitter.
Every word, every gesture, every creation carries frequency.

The twin flame bond was never meant to end in romance;
it was meant to ignite remembrance so powerful it spills into the world.
You start noticing how your presence uplifts others,
how compassion comes more naturally,
how you feel guided to teach, write, heal, or create beauty.
That's the flame doing its work through you.

When you live from that vibration, you no longer need the mirror to reflect it back.
You have become the mirror—steady, luminous, whole.

And if reunion comes, it's not as two halves searching for completion,
but as two sovereign flames walking side by side,
anchoring light where love once burned through illusion.

Because the true union isn't in the meeting of two bodies,
but in the merging of purpose,
where love stops being a feeling and becomes a force.

REFLECTION

Some connections ignite more than emotion,
they awaken direction.

Love stops being a story between two,
and becomes a force moving through you.

Mission energy is love in motion,
the moment affection evolves into purpose.
You begin to sense that the real union
is not just with another soul,
but with the work you came here to do.

Pause and reflect:
What does love want to create through you?
Where is it asking you to serve, to shine, to share?

When love becomes purpose,
every act — no matter how small,
becomes a prayer of remembrance.

Part III

Soulmates & Sacred Companions

Chapter 11

Soulmates: Harmony and Healing

Gentle partnerships for peace

Not every love arrives as a storm.
Some come as a quiet morning;
a hand that fits without effort,
a voice that doesn't ask you to change.

Soulmates are the soft landings
after lifetimes of climbing mountains.
They enter not to awaken the fire,
but to remind you what peace feels like.

These are the gentle partnerships;
healing, balanced, steady.
They don't demand ascension or intensity.
They invite rest.
They teach you that love can be kind.

A soulmate doesn't push your wounds open;
they hold the light while you heal them yourself.
They reflect your goodness,
not your chaos.
Their presence feels like safety,
and in that safety,
your nervous system remembers home.

You don't have to chase a soulmate.
You attract them
when your soul begins to crave calm more than drama,
truth more than spark,
depth more than adrenaline.

They arrive when the heart has learned discernment
that love isn't proven through pain,
but through presence.

With them, conversations feel like exhale.
Silence is not emptiness,
but communion.

Together, you begin to remember
that peace is also passion,
just in a quieter tone.
That healing doesn't have to be hard,
it can happen through laughter,
through dinner shared,
through the comfort of someone simply staying.

Soulmates teach you the art of gentle love,
the kind that mends without noise,
that rebuilds faith in connection.
They are the soul's reward
for every storm it has survived.

REFLECTION

Harmony doesn't mean perfect sameness.
It means two souls learning how to breathe together —
how to listen, soften, and meet halfway.

Every soulmate connection arrives with medicine.
Sometimes the medicine is comfort.
Sometimes it's challenge.
But it always brings you closer to balance within yourself.

Take a moment to ask:
What has this connection taught me about giving and receiving?
Where did I find healing,
and where did I find truth?

Love in harmony isn't about never falling out of tune,
it's about remembering how to return to the song.

Chapter 12

Kindred Spirits

Friendships that feel eternal

Not all soul connections arrive as romance.
Some walk in as laughter.
As effortless conversations.
As the quiet recognition of, "I've known you before."

Kindred spirits are the ones
who remind you that love wears many forms.
They meet you where your soul breathes easiest
without conditions, without contracts,
without the need to fix or prove.

These are the friendships
that feel like home in motion.
Where words are optional
and silence is sacred.

You share stories,
but more than that — you share frequency.
They understand your pauses.
They see the world through a similar lens,
as if remembering a light you both once carried.

Kindred spirits cross paths
when your heart is ready to experience love
without expectation.
They teach that connection doesn't always need a title,
it can simply be.

Sometimes they stay a lifetime.
Sometimes only a season.
But the imprint they leave
is always one of gentle expansion.

You may not speak for years,
and yet when you meet again,
it feels like no time has passed,
because souls don't count in minutes.
They move in resonance.

Kindred spirits are the bridges
between lives, lifetimes, and lessons.
They keep you soft
when the world tries to harden you.
They remind you
that love can be lighthearted and free,
without weight, without agenda —
just presence.

Cherish these connections.
They are proof
that the universe doesn't always send teachers through pain.
Sometimes it sends them through joy.

REFLECTION

Some souls feel like déjà vu,
not because you've met before,
but because they move at the same rhythm.

A kindred spirit doesn't complete you;
they resonate with you.
Their energy hums in the same key,
reminding you that connection can be effortless.

Think of someone whose presence feels easy —
no masks, no tension, no performance.
That comfort is recognition.
It's the soul remembering familiarity in another form.

Cherish those bonds.
They are reminders that not all love burns,

some love simply glows.

Chapter 13

Family as Soul Agreements

The contracts we sign before birth

Before you took your first breath,
you already knew their faces.
You chose them
not by comfort, but by purpose.

Family isn't just blood.
It's a soul curriculum.
Each member plays a role
in the story of your becoming.

Some arrive to love you unconditionally.
Some to challenge you until you remember your strength.
Some to wound you
just enough to open your eyes to truth.

No one appears by accident.
Even the ones who seem hardest to understand
are teachers disguised as parents,
siblings, or children.

You agreed to meet them in this play of time —
to dance through lessons of forgiveness, patience, and compassion.

To test what unconditional love really means
when placed inside a human body.

The soul sees beyond the drama.
It remembers the pact:

"You will forget who I am,
but I will trigger you until you remember."

Some families awaken you through kindness.
Others through contrast.
But all of them serve the same purpose —
to help you recognize your own light
through the mirror of relationship.

When you start seeing your family as sacred agreements,
resentment softens.
You stop asking, "Why did this happen to me?"
and begin whispering, "What was I meant to learn here?"

Forgiveness becomes easier
when you remember the contract.
No longer victims, only actors in a divine rehearsal,
learning how to love even when it hurts.

And one day, when the lesson completes,
you'll look at them and see
not just mother, father, or child,
but fellow souls
walking you home.

REFLECTION

Before you took your first breath,
you chose a circle
not by chance, but by purpose.

Family is not always about likeness;
it's about lessons.
Each soul within it plays a role
in shaping the story you came to live.

Some teach love through presence.
Others teach strength through challenge.
All are agreements written in light,
contracts designed for growth.

Take a moment to reflect:
What did your family come to awaken in you?
What have you learned through them
about forgiveness, resilience, or love?

When you see the soul beneath the role...

even pain becomes sacred.

Chapter 14

Animals and Earth Allies

The non-human soulmates

Not all soulmates walk on two legs.
Some have paws, wings, or roots.
Some speak through silence,
through eyes that understand before words exist.

Animals carry an ancient loyalty,
a frequency unclouded by ego.
They don't care who you've been,
what you've done,
or whether you're healed.
They love from the pure instinct of recognition.

Their souls remember you.
Across lifetimes, across forms.
A dog that finds you in this life
may have stood beside you as a lion,
a bird, or even a guardian in another realm.

When you hold them,
the body relaxes,
the heart softens.
It's because their love vibrates at the rhythm of truth —
no judgment, only being.

And then there are the Earth allies —
trees, oceans, mountains,
the wind that greets you by name.
They, too, are alive with consciousness.
They breathe with you,
respond to your thoughts,
and remember the promises made
between human and planet.

We were never meant to walk this world alone.
The Earth herself volunteered
to be the stage for our evolution;
to hold our tears, absorb our fears,
and sing us back into balance.

Every animal, every element,
is a thread in the great web of remembrance.
They help us return to simplicity;
to love without condition,
to exist without pretense,
to feel without words.

When an animal chooses you,
it's not coincidence.
It's a reunion.
A piece of your soul saying, "I found you again."

So honor them.
Speak to them.
Thank the Earth that holds you both.
Because sometimes,
your greatest soulmate
doesn't speak your language,
they understand your silence.

Reflection

Not all teachers speak in words.
Some walk beside you on four legs,
flutter through your window,
or bloom quietly in sunlight.

Animals and Earth allies carry a purer frequency,
they love without judgment,
listen without needing to reply,
and remind you how simple harmony can be.

When you open your heart to them,
you begin to remember another language —
the language of energy, presence, and trust.

Pause for a moment.
Think of a creature or a place in nature
that has comforted or guided you.
What did it show you about love, patience, or belonging?

The Earth is not separate from your journey.
She is your oldest friend.

Chapter 15

When Soulmates Depart

The sacred goodbye

Every soul connection carries an expiration,
not of love,
but of purpose.

Some come to walk beside you for years.
Others only stay long enough
to open a door inside your heart.

The human part aches to hold on.
The soul only bows.
Because it knows,
what is complete cannot be lost.

When a soulmate departs,
the mind mourns the absence,
but the energy remains.
Their imprint lingers like fragrance,
a whisper that says, "We did what we came to do."

The sacred goodbye is not failure.
It is the honoring of timing.
A release without resentment.
A thank you spoken through tears.

Even endings are holy.
They teach you to trust the flow
instead of clinging to the form.
To remember that love is not possession;
it is permission.
Permission to grow,
to evolve,
to love again in new ways.

Souls don't separate;
they shift positions in the great dance.
Some move to the background
to hold you from afar.
Others reincarnate through new faces,
new chapters,
new vibrations of the same bond.

When you feel the ache of absence,
close your eyes and breathe.
They are still there,
just beyond the veil of sight,
smiling at how beautifully you've continued.

Because real love never dies.
It only changes shape.

So grieve gently.
Bless the path they walked with you.
And let your heart stay open.
For every sacred goodbye
is really a sacred continuation
in another form.

REFLECTION

Love never disappears.
It only changes direction.

What once moved toward one person
can now flow through you
into new moments,
new faces,
new creations.

You cannot lose love
once it has lived inside you.
You can only transform it —
let it breathe again,
let it touch others through your words,
your presence,
your light.

Love doesn't end when a story ends.
It continues...
as you

Part IV

The Monad: The One Soul

Chapter 16

Beyond the Mirror

Remembering the one soul

There comes a point
when the longing quiets.
When you stop searching for "the other"
and begin remembering "the whole."

The twin flame,
the soulmate,
the sacred companion —
all were mirrors
reflecting one truth:
you were never divided.

Beyond the mirror,
there is only light.
One consciousness
playing as two,
then many,
so it could see itself from every angle.

When you meet another soul
and say, "You complete me,"
the Monad smiles.
Because what you're really saying is,
"You reminded me of the part I had forgotten."

The journey through love's faces
is the soul's way of finding its own reflection.
Each person, each bond,
another facet of the One looking back.

Union isn't something you reach,
it's something you remember.
A return to awareness so vast
that you can hold all of it,
the love, the loss, the silence,
and still whisper, "All is me."

The Monad isn't a place.
It's a state of being.
Where your heart and Source heart
beat the same rhythm.
Where you no longer chase light
because you are it.

To live from this space
is to see every face as yours,
every heartbreak as holy,
every reunion as remembrance.

The journey home was never outward.
It was always
a circle returning to its center.

And in that stillness,
you finally realize:
the mirror was never outside you;
it was your own soul
reflecting itself in every form of love.

REFLECTION

The mirror was never meant to hold you forever.
It was meant to show you what you already are.

When you move beyond the reflection,
you stop chasing validation
and start living as wholeness.

The lessons your mirror revealed —
love, pain, longing, surrender
were never about the other.
They were steps toward remembering yourself.

Take a breath and look inward.
What part of you is ready to stand on its own?
What can you now see clearly
without needing anyone else to reflect it?

Beyond the mirror lies freedom,
the place where love no longer seeks a face,
because it has finally found home within.

Chapter 17

Integration of Love

When the two become one

Union isn't a moment —
it's a merging of awareness.
Not "you and I" becoming one,
but remembering
we were never two.

Integration happens slowly.
Like dawn unfolding.
A soft blending
of human and divine,
masculine and feminine,
heaven and Earth.

The mind tries to define it,
but the heart just knows.
It feels like peace.
Like still water
after years of searching for shore.

You begin to see through both eyes at once,
the human that feels,
and the soul that witnesses.
They no longer fight.
They dance.

You begin to see through both eyes at once,
the human that feels,
and the soul that witnesses.
They no longer fight.
They dance.

Integration is not about perfection.
It's about presence.
The ability to sit inside any experience
and say, "This too is part of me."

Every shadow welcomed.
Every fear embraced.
Every heartbreak turned into gold.

The twin flame journey
was never meant to end in possession.
It was meant to end in remembrance —
the realization that your love
was guiding you home to yourself.

When the two become one,
you no longer ask, "Where are they?"
Because you feel them
inside every breath.
Every sunrise.
Every act of kindness you offer the world.

Integration is the quiet victory —
no fireworks,
no announcement.
Just a steady glow
that says,
I have come home.

And once you reach this space,
you no longer need to chase the connection.
You are the connection.
The bridge,
the flame,
the Monad —
living as love embodied.

REFLECTION

Love was never meant to stay outside of you.
It came to be remembered, embodied,
and lived through every breath.

Integration happens quietly,
not through grand gestures,
but in the way you speak,
forgive, and choose peace again and again.

The soul's work isn't to find love;
it's to become it.
To hold compassion for the parts still healing
and tenderness for the ones who once hurt.

Take a slow breath and feel love settle inside your body.
Notice how it feels when you no longer chase it —
when it simply is.

This is what the journey has been leading to:
not the ecstasy of connection,
but the serenity of wholeness.

Chapter 18

The Silence of Union

When words are no longer needed

There comes a moment
when love stops speaking.
Not because it has vanished,
but because it has become everything.

The silence of union
isn't empty,
it's full.
Full of presence so vast
that sound would only break it.

You no longer need to explain,
to reach,
to prove.
The need to be understood dissolves
because understanding has already happened
wordlessly,
through vibration.

This is the sacred quiet
that twin flames and mystics describe —
the pause between heartbeats
where only truth remains.

The silence says:
I know you.
I am you.
There is nothing left to seek.

It's not the silence of distance,
but of union so complete
that language feels too small.
You start to sense the other
in the movement of wind,
in the pulse beneath your own skin.
You realize —
you were never apart.

This silence can feel like death to the mind,
but to the soul, it is rebirth.
It's the return to pure awareness
before thought divided the one into two.

The silence says:
I know you.
I am you.
There is nothing left to seek.

It's not the silence of distance,
but of union so complete
that language feels too small.
You start to sense the other
in the movement of wind,
in the pulse beneath your own skin.
You realize —
you were never apart.

This silence can feel like death to the mind,
but to the soul, it is rebirth.
It's the return to pure awareness
before thought divided the one into two.

REFLECTION

Union is not noise or fireworks.
It is stillness.
The soft hum that remains
when all seeking ends.

In that silence,
love no longer needs to speak,
it simply is.

The soul no longer reaches outward.
It rests in its own rhythm,
complete, steady, and awake.

Take a breath and feel the quiet within you.
This is the space you were always returning to —
the place where longing dissolves
and only peace remains.

Union was never about two becoming one.
It was about remembering
that you already were.

Chapter 19

Embodying the Monad

Love in human form

To embody the Monad
is to walk the Earth
as a living prayer.

No longer seeking heaven above you,
you carry it within.
Every breath,
every gesture,
becomes an act of remembrance.

This is where spirit and matter meet.
Where the light doesn't just descend,
it stays.

You begin to see through the eyes of Source.
Not as someone special,
but as someone awake.
Aware that every person you meet
is another expression of the same soul.

The Monad is not an idea;
it's a state of being.
A consciousness so inclusive
that nothing is outside its love.

It doesn't avoid the world.
It walks right into it —
into traffic, conversations, grocery lines,
and quietly radiates peace.

This is mastery in motion.
Not loud, not grand,
but steady.
The kind of light that doesn't need to prove itself.

Embodying the Monad
isn't about perfection.
It's about honesty.
It's about letting the divine pulse through your flaws
and realizing that even your mistakes
serve the greater remembering.

You don't have to renounce being human.
You sanctify it.
You make the mundane holy.
The laugh, the tear, the touch,
each becomes a doorway to the Infinite.

And one day,
you realize the journey never ended;
it simply turned inward
until you could carry the stars in your chest
and call it ordinary life.

This is what it means
to live as love in form:
to see God in everything,
and everything in God.

Reflection

To embody the Monad
is to live as the bridge between heaven and earth —
a soul remembering itself as Source in motion.

You no longer speak of light;
you are it.
You no longer seek unity;
you live it in every word, thought, and choice.

The Monad is not something you reach;
it is what awakens when separation ends.

Pause and feel your breath.
Each inhale is creation.
Each exhale is surrender.
Together they form the rhythm of oneness.

You are not becoming divine.
You are remembering
that you always were.

Chapter 20

Wholeness

The end of searching

At last,
the heart stops running.
The seeking softens.
And what's left
is stillness.

Wholeness isn't something you find;
it's what remains
when you stop believing you were ever broken.

All your lifetimes,
all your lessons,
were pieces of one vast remembering:
that separation was only a dream.

You searched for love,
only to discover
you were made of it.
You searched for truth,
only to realize
it was the silence behind every question.

Wholeness doesn't mean
you never feel pain.
It means pain no longer defines you.
It passes through
like weather across an open sky.

You stop chasing signs and synchronicities,
because life itself has become the sign.
Every moment,
every breath,
whispers, "I am here. I am whole."

Wholeness is humility —
the knowing that you are Source
and yet still learning to love like a human.
It's grace without grandness,
power without pride.

You look at others
and no longer see "them."
Only reflections
of the same soul exploring itself
in countless expressions.

And when you gaze in the mirror,
you no longer ask, "Who am I?"
You smile,
because you finally remember:
I am all of it.

This is the end of the search —
not a finish line,
but a homecoming.
A quiet realization that the journey
was never to find the light,
but to realize
you have always been it.

REFLECTION

Wholeness isn't a destination;
it's the remembrance that nothing was ever missing.

You searched for completion in others,
in love, in answers, in time —
only to discover that every piece you sought
was already within you.

Wholeness feels like calm.
It's the moment you stop reaching
and simply allow yourself to be.

Take a breath.
Feel how your energy gathers quietly inside your heart.
This is you — undivided, unbroken, infinite.

When you live from wholeness,
you no longer chase healing;
you become the space where healing happens.

Part V

Living the Lesson

Chapter 21

Balancing Polarity

Divine feminine & masculine within

Every soul carries both currents —
the sun and the moon,
the river and the mountain.

The divine feminine is the flow,
the intuition,
the listening.
She feels before she speaks.
She nurtures, receives, and trusts the unseen.

The divine masculine is the structure,
the clarity,
the action.
He protects the vision,
anchors dreams into form,
and moves the energy forward.

When these forces are unbalanced,
we swing between extremes —
too open, and we lose ourselves;
too guarded, and we lose connection.

But when they unite,
life moves with grace.
The heart listens (feminine),
and the soul acts (masculine).
The two become one rhythm —
intuition in motion.

Balancing polarity isn't about gender.
It's energy.
A harmony that lives inside you,
waiting to be tuned.

When the feminine feels safe,
she opens.
When the masculine feels trusted,
he softens.
Together, they create wholeness;
not in theory, but in heartbeat.

This is divine partnership within.
When you learn to mother your own fear
and father your own strength,
you stop searching for balance outside yourself.

The twin flame was never just about another person.
It was your inner marriage
calling to be remembered.

And once you feel that sacred union inside,
everything outside begins to align.

REFLECTION

Light and shadow are not enemies;
they are partners in evolution.

Every soul carries both currents:
the giving and the receiving,
the fire and the stillness,
the divine masculine and the divine feminine.

Balance is not about eliminating one,
it's about letting both move in harmony.

When you resist your opposite, you divide yourself.
When you embrace it, you expand.

Take a quiet breath.
Ask yourself:
Where in my life am I too rigid,
and where am I too yielding?

Polarity exists so that love can find motion.
Balance exists so that love can find peace.

Chapter 22

Healing Attachment

Loving without losing yourself

Love isn't meant to erase you.
It's meant to expand you.

But when the heart has known abandonment or fear,
it learns to cling,
mistaking intensity for safety,
and silence for rejection.

Healing attachment
isn't about becoming detached.
It's about learning to love
without disappearing.

The anxious heart says, "Don't leave me."
The avoidant heart says, "Don't come too close."
Both are just children of fear,
two ways of protecting the same wound:
the fear of being unworthy of love.

True healing begins
when you stop trying to earn love
and start remembering you are it.
When you stop waiting for someone to make you whole
and realize you were never missing any piece.

Healthy love doesn't chase or retreat.
It meets.
It breathes.
It allows two souls to orbit freely
without collapsing into each other.

You can hold space for someone
without holding them hostage.
You can care deeply
without carrying their healing.
That's not coldness,
it's consciousness.

When you heal attachment,
you move from need to nourishment.
From "I can't live without you"
to "I love walking this life with you."

This is mature love —
love with roots and wings.
It honors connection
without sacrificing self.
It trusts that what is meant for you
cannot be lost,
and what leaves
is simply redirecting you toward alignment.

Healing attachment
is the art of staying open
even when afraid.
Of loving fully
while standing in your own light.

Because when love no longer fills a void,
it becomes what it was always meant to be:
a celebration,
not a rescue.

REFLECTION

Attachment begins in fear,
the fear of loss, of distance, of not being enough.
But love that clings cannot breathe.
It must learn to trust its own wings.

Healing attachment doesn't mean closing your heart;
it means opening it wider,
enough to love without control,
to care without needing to possess.

When you stop grasping,
love softens into freedom.
You realize the soul never owned anything;
it only ever experienced everything.

Take a slow breath and notice:
Where do you still hold on too tightly?
Can you let love exist without your hands around it?

Healing attachment is remembering
that love was never meant to be held —

only shared.

Chapter 23

The Path of Surrender

From control to trust

Surrender isn't giving up.
It's giving over.
Not to fate,
but to flow.

The mind wants to know.
It wants timelines, outcomes, and certainty.
But love, purpose, awakening;
they all bloom in mystery.

Surrender is the bridge between human will
and divine orchestration.
It's the moment you stop pushing the river
and realize you are the river.

Control comes from fear,
the fear that if you don't hold on,
everything will fall apart.
But the truth is,
the tighter you grip,
the less you can receive.

The universe doesn't respond to pressure.
It responds to openness.
It moves through the space
you create when you let go.

To surrender
is to trust that life is intelligent.
That love knows its way home
without your constant supervision.

It doesn't mean you stop caring,
it means you stop forcing.
You keep showing up,
but you release the need
to decide how things should unfold.

Every unanswered prayer,
every delay,
every detour
is love in disguise,
redirecting you to what aligns
with who you're becoming.

When you truly surrender,
you don't lose power.
You merge with a greater one.
You start to move
with the rhythm of creation itself.

And suddenly, what once felt uncertain
becomes effortless.
Because the moment you trust the current,
the current carries you.

Surrender isn't the end of control,
it's the beginning of peace.

Surrender isn't something that happens all at once.
It unfolds in small moments, quiet recognitions that you no longer need to fight what life is showing you.
You start to soften, to breathe differently, to listen instead of resist.
This isn't defeat, it's alignment.
It's how the heart learns to trust again, not through control, but through allowing.

Here are a few ways you can tell you're surrendering, not giving up:

1. You feel peace, not apathy.
2. You're no longer fighting the current, but you still care deeply, just without control.
3. You stop chasing clarity and start trusting timing.
4. You know answers arrive when your energy is ready, not when your mind demands.
5. You release expectations, but not faith.
6. You still believe in love, purpose, and healing, even if you can't predict how.
7. You let yourself rest.
8. You understand that pausing isn't weakness; it's integration.
9. You speak softly to yourself.
10. The inner critic grows quiet, replaced by patience and self-compassion.

11. You're guided by feeling, not fear.
12. You make choices from peace, not panic.
13. You stop replaying the past.
14. You bless it, thank it, and move forward lighter.
15. You still show up, just differently.
16. Instead of grasping, you open.
    Instead of pushing, you allow.
17. You begin to notice beauty again.
18. Even small things — sunlight, laughter, stillness, remind you that life continues to love you.
19. You feel connected, even alone.
20. Because you realize surrender isn't losing someone, it's finding yourself.

Reflection

Surrender is not weakness;
it is strength in its purest form.

It is the moment the soul whispers,
"I trust what I cannot control."

When you stop fighting the current,
life begins to carry you
to places your mind could never plan.

Surrender is not giving up,
it is giving over,
handing your story back to the divine
and saying, "Lead me."

Take a gentle breath.
What are you still trying to hold together?
What could unfold if you allowed life to move freely through you?

The path of surrender is where peace begins,
not in answers, but in trust.

Chapter 24

Reunion Through Self-Love

Coming home to your own heart

Every search for love
is really a search for home.
We spend lifetimes looking outward
for the one who will see us,
choose us,
stay.

But the great reunion
was never between two bodies.
It was between you
and your own heart.

Self-love isn't a slogan.
It's a practice of returning.
Returning to the parts of you
you once abandoned
to be accepted.
The softness you hid,
the voice you silenced,
the dreams you postponed
so others would feel comfortable.

Real self-love is radical remembering
that you were worthy before you achieved anything,
beautiful before anyone said so,
whole before anyone arrived.

When you turn inward with tenderness,
the ache begins to dissolve.
You stop begging for crumbs
because you finally realize
you are the feast.

This is the reunion
when the divine within
meets the human who forgot.
When the child inside you
feels seen,
safe,
and loved at last.

You start giving yourself
the things you once demanded from others —
attention, honesty, consistency, care.
And love that once felt like survival
becomes creation.

Every time you choose yourself with kindness,
you rewire lifetimes of longing.
You teach the universe
how to treat you.

The twin flame,
the soulmate,
the companion —
they were mirrors
guiding you back to this moment.

Because the real union
was never about finding them.
It was about finding you.

And when you come home to your heart,
you stop chasing love...

you become it.

Reflection

Reunion doesn't always happen between two souls.
Sometimes it happens within,
when every part of you finally feels safe to return home.

Self-love is not vanity.
It is remembrance.
It is the moment you stop looking for love in reflection
and start radiating it from your own heart.

Each time you forgive yourself,
each time you choose gentleness instead of judgment,
you move closer to wholeness.

Pause for a moment.
Place a hand over your heart.
Ask softly: What does my soul need from me today?

Reunion begins when you become
the love you once hoped to find.

Chapter 25

Beyond Reunion

Living the mission

The journey was never just about union.
It was preparation.

Every heartbreak,
every awakening,
every moment of silence.
it was shaping you
into a vessel for love in action.

Beyond reunion,
love stops being personal.
It becomes purpose.

You begin to understand
that what you feel as "my mission"
is really love wanting to move through you:
in words, in work, in presence.

You no longer ask,
"What am I here to get?"
but,
"What am I here to give?"

Mission doesn't always look grand.
Sometimes it's a quiet kindness,
a message that reaches one person at the right time,
a vibration that steadies a room.
You start to realize
your energy is the message.

To live the mission
is to embody what you've learned —
to love without agenda,
to walk in integrity,
to let your peace become your teaching.

You stop waiting for the perfect moment.
You understand that life itself
was the initiation.

This is mastery;
not the end of the path,
but its flowering.
Where love no longer seeks union,
because it has become union.

Your story becomes service.
Your light becomes language.
And your presence,
a silent reminder to others
of what they already are.

You came to remember.
Now you are here to radiate.

Beyond reunion,
there is only love
living through you,

as you,

for all.

REFLECTION

Reunion was never the end.
it was the beginning of remembrance.

When love expands beyond two,
it becomes purpose.
When purpose expands beyond self,
it becomes service.

Living the mission means walking as love in motion,
anchoring light through ordinary moments,
turning kindness into frequency,
and creation into prayer.

Take a quiet breath.
Ask your soul: How does love wish to move through me now?
Let the answer be simple — a smile, a word, a gesture.

You are the embodiment of every lesson,
every mirror, every awakening.
This is the life where love becomes form.
This is the moment the Monad breathes through you.

FINAL REFLECTION

Final Reflection

Love as Remembrance

In the end,
it was never about finding the other.
It was about remembering the One.

Love was never something to earn.
It was the thread that wove every lesson,
every loss,
every miracle together.

The twin flame taught you fire.
The soulmates taught you peace.
The Monad taught you wholeness.
And life...
life taught you how to live it all.

Every chapter of your story
was love wearing a different costume,
whispering the same truth:
You are not separate from what you seek.

When you live from that remembrance,
every encounter becomes sacred.
Every breath becomes prayer.
And every moment,
an invitation to be love made visible.

So walk gently now.
You don't have to prove or pursue.
Just keep becoming
what you already are.

Because the greatest teaching
was never in the meeting or the merging;
it was in the remembering.

Love was the beginning.
Love was the path.
Love is what remains.

Afterword Reflection

The silence after love speaks

There comes a moment when there's nothing left to seek.
No more questions to ask,
no more lessons to chase.

Only a soft knowing remains —
that love was never something you found,
but something you became.

You've walked through longing and letting go,
through union and remembrance.
Now you stand in the gentle truth:
you were always whole.

Let this silence be your teacher now.
Sit in it the way light sits in space
without effort, without need.

And when you rise,
let your life be the remembrance .

EPILOGUE

The Return Home

In the end, love was never asking you to chase.
It was asking you to remember.

Every connection, every ache, every miracle,
was guiding you inward,
back to the quiet center of your being
where separation never existed.

You came to Earth to rediscover what you already are:
the embodiment of divine love
learning to see itself through human eyes.

When you understand this,
you stop searching for the one
and start being the one —
the one who loves, who forgives, who creates.

The path of the Monad is simple.
It is the journey from I love you
to I am love.
And in that silence, Love looked upon itself ,
and remembered it was One.

www.ingramcontent.com/pod-product-compliance
Lightning Source LLC
Chambersburg PA
CBHW071208070526
44584CB00019B/2955